A Simple Smile

DOROTHY MAHFOOD

ROCKSTONE
PUBLISHING
HOUSE

© Dorothy Mahfood 2020

No part of this publication may be altered, reproduced, distributed, or transmitted in any form, by any means, including, but not limited to, scanning, duplicating, uploading, hosting, distributing, or reselling, without the express prior written permission of the publisher, except in the case of reasonable quotations in features such as reviews, interviews, and certain other non-commercial uses currently permitted by copyright law.

This poetic memoir is a work of creative nonfiction. While some factual details have been embellished or altered for literary effect, all of the events are true to the best of the poet's recollection. All opinions expressed in this book are the poet's or fictional.

A Simple Smile by Dorothy Mahfood

Rockstone Publishing House
ISBN: 978-1-7359083-1-1

Contents

Forward..1
Intro 5
A Poet I Shall Be 7
Jamaica..9
Beckoning Memories (Jamaica) 11
Drawing Me Back (Land of My Birth) 11
The Wicked City, 1692... 14
Nuh Tru 15
Man, Nuh Badda Mi.. 16
Family..19
A Simple Smile.. 21
Born on a Horse... 22
Mass Willie and Cissy 25
The Next Birthday 29
The Feather Pen 30
Under a Rock... 31
Motherhood (An Amazing Blessing)..................... 33
The Lost Key.. 35
His Journey Home (My Vision) 35
The Chi Chi Bird's Song...................................... 38
A Simple Smile (Afterward).................................. 40

Home 43

World War II (History) 45
The Old Water Drip 46
Separator and Old Butter Churn 47
Bluefields Guest House 48

Nature 51

My Palomino 53
Mules 55
Seen Things Few Have Ever Seen 56
Open Your Eyes 57
Amazing God I Love 58
Alone 60
After a Hurricane 61
Icefield Parkway 62
Black Bears (an Icefield Excursion) 64

Un-Nature 67

Selfie Generation 69
I Do Not Understand. Do You? 70
The Flood 71
Alone, Yet Not Alone 71

God 73

One Slip Away 75
More Like You 76
Storms 77
Wisdom 78
The Old Master and His Masterpiece 79
Unfolding Rosebud 80

Knitting 81
Redeeming Grace, I Could Not Claim 82

Growing Old **85**

Legs 87
Glacial Flow (Slowing Down) 88
Lungs 88
The Dripping Faucet 89
Teach Us, Nuh Man! 91
Reflect on Him 92

Outro **95**

The Rose 97

Inspired by Dorothy's Life **99**
Oristano **101**

Forward

Born in 1934 at Shafston, a great house in the parish of Westmoreland, Jamaica, Dorothy Mahfood, my mother, grew up with a love for nature—birds, goats, soldier crabs, her Palomino horse. Rather than sewing with her mother and two sisters, she preferred adventures with her brothers on their father's extensive property or down in the small coastal village of Bluefields.

In her teen years she boarded at Hampton School in the Santa Cruz Mountains where her sisters also attended school. While there she joined the field hockey team, playing center back as she wasn't afraid to defend her goal by tackling her opponents. She was also appointed as a prefect over the younger Hampton girls. After high school she returned home and, realizing there were no opportunities for her there, took a job with a tour company in Kingston. She worked her way up to become the company's Kingston airport representative where she had the privilege of meeting many famous people. During those times, she was introduced to my father, Kenneth Mahfood, at the happening Kingston night club, the Glass Bucket. Two years later they married.

The two worked well together in business, with my father's thorough caution and my mother's calculated risk. Over the years they began two car-rental agencies—one became a Hertz Car Rental franchise and the other a National Car Rental franchise. During the first car-rental agency era, my siblings, Jo Anne and Bruce, and I were born.

After starting the second car-rental business, a friend introduced my mother to the game of golf. As is her way with all things, she practiced hard, hitting thousands of balls a day before or after work. It's no wonder she eventually became the first woman to win the Caribbean Golf Championship. She then represented Jamaica in the Women's World Cup of Golf. This was during the 1970s when the political climate in Jamaica was unstable. Many Jamaicans were leaving the country, and my parents did the same. We moved to Florida where my mother built a successful career as a real-estate agent.

I won't detail every step of my mother's life from that point forward, except to say that whatever she puts her hand to she thrives at. On top of her previously mentioned accomplishments, she is a gardener, a seamstress, an artist, a photographer, and most recently, a poet.

It's a funny story how the poetry thing happened. Knowing she could master writing as she had other things, I asked her to join a writing group I was starting. She said she'd think about it. That night, on her own, she decided she'd try her hand at poetry and wrote what is now the title poem of this book, "A Simple Smile." The next day she said to me, "I'm quitting the writing group!" I told her she couldn't quit something she'd never joined. Then she read me the poem. That's my mother! Always joking around; always excelling at everything. From that point on, she used poetry as a vehicle to record many aspects of her life, particularly the early days on her father's property.

The poems in this collection are grouped thematically, but if read from start to finish, there is a loose chronology to them. I pray you enjoy these poems as they give you a glimpse into the life of an incredible woman!

—Dale Mahfood

Intro

A Poet I Shall Be

I will scratch and claw
I will fight my way
Even if it hurts my paw
I will pen a line each day
—A poet I will be

Should I fall along the road
Get up, I will, and fetch my load
With open eye and ear
Consider the path of the deer
Because a poet I shall be

God's creatures great and small
I carefully track them all
I study their every move
In them the perfection I see
Of the amazing God I love

My goal! A famous poet I will be
Should I fall along the road
Get up, I will and fetch my load
I'll not relent as I travel on this road
Because—a poet I shall be!

Jamaica

Beckoning Memories (Jamaica)

Beckoning memories fill my soul
Of that lovely land called home
No matter which path life leads me down
I never forget those days—
Those days of old—no longer
Oh, how my love grows fonder the more I ponder
Your precious memories overflowing as waterfalls
Land of my birth, I hear your calls

Drawing Me Back (Land of My Birth)

Jamaica, Jamaica, the land of my birth
Memories that constantly flow
Not unlike your rhythms and rhymes
I wish for these times so

Life's journey took me far away
To a life so different from yours
Yet, I gladly admit these old-time memories
Draw me back to your blessed shores

A Jewel in the emerald waters
Of the Caribbean Sea
Pristine beauty of your open lands
Sugarcane flowing in the breeze

Many rivers, magnificent falls
Trees and fruits in abundant supply
Towering Blue Mountains piercing the clouds
Climbing to reach the skies

Your people are like none other on earth
All gets done, but not in a rush
The laid-back way of life—no problem, man
It's like living a royal flush:

Peanut man with whistle attached to his cart
Selling pepper "swimp" and boiled peanuts in a brown paper bag

Another man with a cart shouting:
Icicles, ice cream, fudge on a likkle stick, grater cake,
Paradise plumb, John Bailey, coconut drop
Bruck-me-jaw, sweetie, bulla, and gizzarda
One shilling coco-bread and hot patty
Six-pence "aerated water" with Busta Backbone

A man with a basket on back of his motorcycle yelling:
Oysters and pepper sauce! I wil' open dem fi y'u

Jerk pork to make you tongue fly out you mouth
If you're in the country parts, Boston Bay is de place
In Kingston, Speedy Jerk Shop—best jerk pork ever

Half Way Tree, near the clock
The famous Glass Bucket—dancing to the ska,
Rock and roll, rock-steady, reggae, soul, and calypso
Played by Carlos Malcolm and the Vikings
And famous Byron Lee and the Dragonaires

Dressing up, jacket and tie to Carib Theatre on a Saturday night
The iconic Myrtle Bank Hotel patronised by society's elite
Weddings and new year's balls held there
Motor race at Vernam Field, May Pen
Cheering my old school in the Manning's Cup

Listening to a little Rediffusion soundbox
Catching waves from Radio Jamaica's one station
Popular radio soap opera, *Dulcimina*
Watching a lone black-and-white TV channel—JBC
Radio announcer Charles Babcock, self-named "The Cool Fool"

Department stores: Nathan's, Times Store, London Shop, and Issa's
King Street open-air market on Christmas Eve
Shoppers dressed in their best
Mad rush to get things done

I thank the Lord I was born in this paradise
I love you, Jamaica, my emerald in the sun

Yeah, man, de ole-time days was de bes'
I wish ole-time everyt'ing would a neva dun!

The Wicked City, 1692

British pirates roamed the seas
Then anchored for a time of wild frolicking
Bars and brothels occupied every corner
Of this busiest and wealthiest Caribbean port
The little church Sunday service was over,
A minister had preached, then closed the door
He was seen entering the Ram Goat Pub

Wine goblet in hand he took a swig
The earth shook, buildings were quickly falling
He saw the city disappearing into the ocean
Hundreds of ships sinking under tsunami waves
To become the richest repository of historic shipwrecks
Thousands of people drowned that day
Two-thirds of this wicked city sank beneath the sea

Madness now living within his mind as he thought,
Could I be drunk after just one sip?
His head possessed with thoughts of unbelief
He turned—the city had sunk on that side too
Dropping the goblet, the wine spilled
There was nowhere to run. Then it was over

Calm again, the earth shook no more

The minister and other fortunate souls stood speechless
A narrow strip of land and a third of the city left behind
The church stood firm, untouched by this ordeal
Left to tell the stories of those wicked days
Are twisted buildings and damage everywhere

The old fort now a place where visitors imagine a time
When pirates ruled the waves, and contemplate
What it was like for the minister seeing all he saw that day.
The wrath of God poured out on Port Royal, June 7th, 1692

Nuh Tru

A go Jamaica de odder day
Mi fren' was tellin' me seh das one nodda fren', Miss Kitty
Was comin' by fi seh 'owdy[1] to mi

---

[1] 'owdy – While speaking, Jamaicans often drop the "h" at the beginning of a word (so *howdy* becomes *'owdy*). We also tend to add an "h" to other words that don't have one (so *and* becomes *hand*). There is a well-known Jamaican saying that illustrates this well: "Teacher, *'Arry* take the *'ammer* and

Han'[1] shi tell 'ar sey das shi 'ave a fren' wid 'ar

So me tell 'ar to hinvite de two a dem fi cum ober an nyam[2] some bickle[3] wid us
Mi tell 'ar das me was glad fi 'ear she was comin fi see mi
But was to memba seh das Kitty nyam nuff[4] food
So wi 'ave fi cook plenty heckstra

Me frien' suck 'ar teet', an' tell mi seh, "Nuh true?"

Man, Nuh Badda Mi

A wha yu a as' me seh?
Weh you kan buy 'ardoe bread[5]
Han' cow milk fi de pickney[6] dem?
Wha part de shop de?
Wife a sleep and di pickney a ball

Nuh badder mi, fa mi nuh go deer
Mi live hover suh; no need no milk

'it me on me *'ead!*" To which the teacher replies, "*hemphasize* your *haitches* you *hignorant hidiot!*"

[2] nyam: eat
[3] bickle - food
[4] nuff - a lot
[5] hard dough bread – a slightly sweet dense Jamaican bread
[6] pickney - children

'Ave mi hown cow hover a mi yard
Get nuf milk a mornin' time
Han' me no need no 'ardoe bread

Mi Pinckney dem get up hearly
Han' go milk cow, den dem go a school
Me go grung[7] an' plant yam an t'ing
Nu more question, cause me gone a grung
Suh, nuh badda me, far mi busy

---

[7] grung - ground

Family

A Simple Smile

The woman I call Mother
This little lady was never a bother
The sacrifices for her five untold
Her patience, a model to behold
She never wavered from her smile
I love your smile, Mother

Your silent endurance and steadfast love
Shown to me through your loving smile
I was young and didn't understand
The sad times hid behind that simple expression
Strength so obvious through a beaming face
You sacrificed so a normal childhood we could have

You taught me how to knit and sew
Which has saved a fortune as my children grew
This gift of joy received from you
Taught me happiness when things go wrong
Much gained from that enduring smile

There was a time when I thought you were so weak
How could you concede to trials you often faced?
These times made my anger boil
You should fight back hard, I thought
I wanted to take over and fight your fight
Instead, you loved me with your protective smile

We five left the nest and went our way
But only to return and whisk you away
Abused no more, an unhappy, silent past left behind
You brought with you a joyful heart
It was our crown to give you happiness until your end
We enjoyed you, Mother

God gave you a silent, golden strength
The rays that glittered from your smile
Now shine on me today
You gave me everything; you gave me life
I smile and say, "God filled me with her strength"
I love you, Mother

Born on a Horse

I was three when my father put me on a donkey
Quite young when I began to ride alone
Ridden goats, cows, donkeys, mules, horses
I even rode a pig one day
The smoothest ride of all—the mule, for sure
Rode standing on a horse; lay on the back of a donkey
As he walked down a steep incline

Thrown from a horse galloping under a pimento tree
A branch took me to the ground
Threw me into a pile of stones and nettles
I quickly got up and ran after the horse

Mounted him again and off we went

Swam in the ocean with my horse
Under unlimited blue skies
On Sundays, rode by myself to church
Hardly a day went by I did not ride
Never liked to repeat a track
There was always an adventure on a new path

At seventeen I got a job with a tour company
Which was on Harbour Street in Kingston
I heard about the horses at a racetrack
One day after work, I went to inquire
Here I introduced myself to the stable owner
And asked him if I could ride one of his horses

He replied, "These are racehorses. You can't ride them"
I answered, "I know how to ride." But again, he echoed,
"My child, you don't understand; these horses are racehorses
You are at Knutsford Park and over there is the racetrack
Do you want to get killed?"

I quietly replied, "Sir, I won't get killed, I was born on a horse
I have even broken in young, wild colts for riding myself

I can ride your horses if you will let me"

With that, he called the attendant, who brought out a horse
He told me, "Go ride and let me decide"
At the gate, I mounted this gorgeous, well-kept animal
He was washed and groomed and precisely shod
For a moment I thought I was in a wild dream
Then my thoughts brought me back to the track

As the gate opened the horse jumped forward
In a flash we galloped around Knutsford Park racetrack
Wow! Could he move. It was the fastest I had ever been
I was excited—exhilarated—and in my element
I'm here riding a racehorse, the dream of a lifetime
My brothers will be jealous when I tell them

Every evening after work, I would help exercise a horse or two
Adventures have never been rare for me
But this was truly an experience never to be forgotten:
The wind blowing in my face as I galloped around the track
"I see such joy in your smile as you fly past the gate," the stable owner said
Thank you Mr. Zaide for believing in me
A girl from Westmoreland—born on a horse

Mass Willie and Cissy

William James Hylton Cooke and Elianora Sarah McCall Cooke (Nee Grange), "Mass Willie and Cissy"

Part I

A jolly old man and his wife Cissy
In their nineties still holding hands
They were my awesome grandparents
Most would wish they had
He sat on his veranda chair
Pipe in hand, matches strewn around on the floor

They lived in a six-bedroom house called Lennox
In the parish of Westmoreland, Jamaica
A mischievous smile had he
We called him Mass Willie
I loved him, he was so silly

The only time he didn't joke—
"Silence!" World War II news
A boring time for me
Thirty minutes seemed so long
A serious listening time for him
The old radio, BBC turned on

Granny taught me to crochet, knit, and tat
On her veranda chair she sat
Knitting phenomenal wool sweaters

A personal generous way of serving
Men she never knew
They were soldiers in World War II

We helped pack boxes of sweaters
That were mailed to the UK armed forces
Distributed to the men fighting for our freedom

Two visiting rules I must obey
Wear a dress—no slacks allowed
Ride the horse sidesaddle
Out of sight, I disobeyed!
I arrived one day in slacks
Only to remain in the car for hours
While my mother and Granny visited
Obedience quickly learned

Part II

Mass Willie loved wildlife of all kinds
He had chickens, ducks, geese, swans, peafowl, to name a few
Pigeons nesting everywhere
Roosters crowing early, awaking us
Guinea fowl, the watchdog of them all
Perched high in his breadfruit trees
After dark anyone approaching
A short, quick, loud and constant chirping noise was heard

Signalling someone was drawing near

With radiant enjoyment on Mass Willie's face
The parrot sang, "It's a long way to Tipperary"
It knew the entire song
Mass Willie even taught it how to
Tell the dog to chase approachers
"Sic him, Timmy!" the parrot shouted, then laughed with glee
Vacations at my grandparents' were such a blast

Eleven a.m. the *Daily Gleaner* car came around the bend, honking its horn!
Time for the gardener to fetch the newspaper dropped off at the gate

A bell rang, the signal for washing hands
The second ring meant to be at the table without delay
Sit up straight, no elbows on the table
Use your knife and fork, small portions on your plate
Hard to do, as curdle-sauce chicken was passed around!
Made with corn-fed chicken and fresh eggs

After lunch each day, Mass Willie's pet lizard
Came crawling down the old patio post
Climbed on his wooden armchair and shared his ginger sugar

Feeding these birds and creatures was a special joy for me
A time engraved in my very soul
My grandpa taught me to love them all

Part III

From the veranda looking across the garden
A narrow road led to a small church perched on the distant hill
I often wondered what it was like to visit there
My grandparents didn't go to church anymore
In their nineties, it was painful to get around

I picked four-o'clocks for Grannie to enjoy
Pink and white flowers placed in a tiny straw basket
Then presented them to her as a surprise!
No substitute for this special time
I can't explain the joy I felt to see her smile
My love for both of them, so deep
My grandparents! My delight!

With moon shadows creeping across the floor
Eyelids heavy as weights
My siblings and I
Bid Mass Willie and Cissy goodnight
And headed to bed without a fight

The Next Birthday

Grandpa called his chauffeur, "Web!
It's Miss Dorothy's birthday today
Get the car ready for Shafston"
Living in the Lennox servants' quarters
Driving Mass Willie, Cissy, and Auntie Gladys
Web and the 1927 black Ford
Never missed one of our birthdays
Our only visitors, a telegram apprised us of their arrival

An hour's journey, Web and his passengers
Ascended the mile drive to Shafston
Honking the horn at intervals along the way
Echoing their arrival up pasture lands
As we perched on the veranda railing
Our ears transfixed on the valley below

At the first honk, off the railing we jumped
Jostling out the front door
Running down the gravel road until we met the car
Web stopped, and on to the running boards we jumped
Holding on by the window frame
Our gleeful voices muted out of respect for our aged grandparents

I loved when they came to visit

Arriving at three-thirty sharp, tea was served at four
Crustless sandwiches, milk-poured-first English tea,
    and a birthday cake
Icing made of butter, powdered sugar, and egg whites
Mortar and pestled until the icing thickened
Spread on a round pound cake and left to harden
For me, the icing was the whole point!

Mass Willie kept us enthralled with stories, jokes
And his tobacco-stained finger in his pipe
Pressing the hot tobacco
I don't remember my father at our birthday parties
My older sister, Maggie, confirmed that fact
I never gave it a thought—it was the norm
Mass Willie was always there, though, and in rare form

Five-thirty, their departure time
To make it home before dark
Hunched over the veranda railing
We watched Web and Grandpa's Ford
Disappear down the gravel road

"When's the next birthday?"

The Feather Pen

A plucked feather from the wing
Of Grandpa's swan

One squawk and she was gone
My heart pounded as I hurried
To show the treasure I had won

Mother! The inkpot? The inkpot?
Clean the feather, make the quill
Don't mess your dress, keep still
Don't spill the priceless ink
Fill the inkpot over the sink

Grandpa is out with his chickens
He'll be surprised when he returns
Today is his ninetieth birthday
I will pen him with this special quill
My joy, his heart to fill

Under a Rock

Young and fearless—
Adventures for me, never rare
My sisters only sat sewing
Such a waste!
I'd rather take a dare

"What shall we do today?"
My brothers would say
Something different, not just play
Down the hill we ran, across the cow pen

Up another hill we climbed
The peak covered with trees
Rocks large and small everywhere

"Check the trees for birds who nest"
Empty nests found way up high
On the ground I turned over a rock
"Something moved," I cried
It quickly slid away

From a branch my older brother jumped
And rolled away a large rock
Under which tiny soldier crabs curled in their shells
"A container, did anyone bring?"
A small bag for specimens was always at my side

Into my bag they were quickly placed
Down the hill and up to home we ran
My brothers had a happy plan
To make a chalk circle on the old red tile
Crabs in the center under a pan

By markings, we three chose each a crab
"First across the circle will be the champ!"
Two sisters not allowed to join the game
These crabs were not theirs to share
They shouted, "That's not fair!"

Our mother appeared to plead their case

"No! They are not allowed to join our game
Unless, of course we can make a deal"
Finally, the deal was made
A loan of two crabs to play
For their share of fried plantain that day

Motherhood (An Amazing Blessing)

Being a great mother is not a skill that can be acquired at university
Nor is it learned from a book or measured by a salary
Yet, being a great mom is the single most important sacrifice
Any woman can contribute to the human race
Yes! It was God's plan from the beginning to multiply and fill the earth

At the birth of a child, a woman is transformed in inexplicable ways
When she holds that little one in her arms for the first time
She receives, it seems to me
A force so powerful, a love so valuable, a gift so lasting
And an enduring strength that allows her to handle
Any and all problems that arise during her life with that child

Children are loaned to us by God; we have the weighty responsibility

Of making sure they grow to be disciplined, responsible adults
Who prayerfully will make a difference in the world
When my children were young they tangled my feet
When they became teens they messed with my heart
We need the fruit of the Spirit at these crucial times

I had a child who had to be completely transfused at birth
I spent numberless, sleepless nights in hospitals and at home
He kept us busy his early years, with croup and asthma he despaired
My husband and I spent many nights on our knees praying for guidance
God gave me a strength that passes all understanding
I could not have had such self-control without the Lord

Little did I know that I would need this strength in the years ahead
The teen years! Be ready! These years will come
It was a challenge to balance work, motherhood, broken bones
The teacher they didn't like, fights with the cousins next door
Teaching them to apologize and to respect older folk
Oh, the sleepless nights—only with God did we get through those days

I am thankful to God and honored that he allowed me
   to be a mother
I love being a mother, mother-in-law, grandmother
   and, now, a great-grandmother!

The Lost Key

We were happy, then suddenly so sad
We couldn't get into the house
Teenagers awake in the backseat
Were as quiet as a mouse
The key was lost and yet to be found
Some thought it might have fallen on the ground
We searched and searched all around

The scorching heat made us weak
Hopeless, we could not find the key
Desperately a sister to the rescue was called
In a rush she finished her work
While we waited in the shade of a guango tree
Watching the road for her car to appear
Now here she is with the lost key!

His Journey Home (My Vision)

I looked—a vision
A donkey leaving a large shade of trees

Growing at the foot of a mountain
He started walking on a narrow footpath
Leading up and across the hills
Every movement seemed painfully slow
The vision soon disappeared

Weeks later, the donkey reappeared walking
Not far up the zigzag mountain path
All around seemed so familiar to me
A few months went—I kept seeing this vision
So constant and in full view
Somehow, I was very much a part of this strange scene

It became more and more real to me
What did this donkey have to do with anything?
The large, shade trees now left behind, faded from sight
The donkey's movement and the path held my focus
Now a part of this strange ordeal
I wondered, Why does he slowly ascend the hill?

The path made a hairpin turn, then ascended
Continuing the zigzag journey—
On a particular day, the rest of the path was in full view
He was noticeably tired and weak
Half-closed eyes and flopping ears
Told me he couldn't make it to the top
I pondered this

One day, the donkey looked quite old
He was tired and worn from his ordeal
He was getting frightfully thin and slow
I had never seen him eat or drink anything
How can he ever make it to the top?
His ears drooped and flopped
His head no longer held up high,
Why does he continue on this trek?

My eyes followed the path to the peak
Why does he want to reach the top?
It makes absolutely no sense at all
He can't make it, he's too weak and frail
Shade he could have, in the trees below
Concerned, I decided I must know
What's up there? What's over the top?
Each day I look intently at the mountain

Saddened, one day I raised my eyes above
Then saw a golden light filling the sky
A sunset, maybe, entered my mind
Suddenly in a flash, a new vision filled my eyes
I found myself looking down the other side of the mountain
That he was so determined to climb
I will try to describe what I saw and felt
Though words are inadequate

The mountainside flowed into a valley below

In the distance, a blinding light came from
An extremely large ball resembling the sun
Light streamed in every direction
Filling all the earth and overwhelming the sky
It was difficult to see; the light was so very bright
Enveloped in by this awe-filled scene
I was allowed to see enough to understand

Clearly, he is headed for this light
I thought, He cannot make this on his own
He has one more turn to make. Maybe I can help
I turned, looking along his path
He was gone! No longer a vision to be seen
A thought came rushing to my mind
God was always there, helping him on his climb
Then carried him over the top to His light far away

I was numb and could not speak
Tears flowed down my cheeks
No words invented can explain this grief
Yet, ineffable joy was given me
So I knew without a doubt, He cares for His own
Now living with Jesus, our Lord and Savior
—My husband died that day

The Chi Chi Bird's Song

Grass looks greener on the other side
Look up and take it in your stride

Advice—Don't go off the path you're on
Unwise think they know what they want
Wise ones know what they don't want

Don't let the storm cloud hide your sky
Look up, focus on the endless light
I'll be there waiting with our Lord and Christ
For each and every one of you
You'll never ever be out of my sight

It was amazing grace that gave me love
For such a brood as you
A privilege to hold you tight to my chest
And listen to your hearts beat as you slept
Each one similar, yet so distinct

First there was Jo Anne—arrived nine days late
Princess of them all, head of hair and energy galore
Along came Bruce, a skinny one was he
No hair on his head, as it had to be shaved
Dale arrived—a blood transfusion causing joyous confusion

I loved you all then with my heart and soul
Today I love each of you with the love of our Lord
Just remember this, when I am gone to be with Him
And you hear a chi chi bird's melodious song,
It's my whisper—remember, you are dearly loved

A Simple Smile (Afterward)

As I read what I had penned, my mind returned to Shafston
I try to imagine what it was like for you after we were all gone
Nothing pleasant comes to mind, though I am now eighty-three
I was seventeen when I left, yet it's still difficult when I think of you
You had to have felt lonely and hopeless

How could we ever help? must have crossed your mind
We left home with only the clothes that you sewed for us
You never shared what it was like; yet, it was a terrible time, I know
Up on the mountaintop; no form of transport; you were stuck
Brought his mistress in to live, redecorated her area like a palace

You resigned yourself to your room all alone with no love
You hid it all behind your silent strength and a constant smile
I struggled for some three years, yet I got my young brother a job
The next year I took my older brother and sent him away

To England, where he joined the British Marines—he
    was safe

Later, Jean and I went to Shafston and snatched you
    away
You were so afraid and did not think you should leave
This time we definitely did not listen to what you said
We knew that you were going with us—and that was
    that
God blessed the rest of your days with much love from
    us five
And your beloved twelve grandchildren, your delight
    and crown

I refused to look at you in your coffin
So glad I didn't—it is not a memory I will ever have
The last time I saw you, you were smiling
That's how I will always remember you
I love you, my precious Mother

Home

World War II (History)

April 30, 1945, "Hitler commits suicide"
I was eleven and standing on the Shafston veranda
Looking down over the Bluefields Bay
The radio turned on

Mother always listened to the news
She shouted from her chair
"The war is over! Thank the Lord!"
The servants came rushing in
The news was blasting loud and clear
Excitement filled the air
Celebration everywhere

I never liked listening to the news
And I didn't understand the war
Silence was expected; I was bored
But now, seeing the excitement all around,
It seemed to mean so much

Suddenly, something seemed special
It left an incredible impression
Winston Churchill and Eisenhower
Became my two heroes
They taught me to love history

The Old Water Drip

Growing up there was no electric, no running water
Only an eight-foot-deep, in-ground swimming-pool-sized tank
Where water was stored and filled by gutters
Spanning the large roof of our country home
Water used for cooking, cleaning, bathing, and all else

In a cool room under the house—the drip room
Stood a drip stone, a large sandstone
—A heavy sandstone, over three feet tall
Its sides and center were smoothly shaped
To fit the stand and be filled with buckets of tank water

This stone was lifted by several hands, then
Placed on the rustic-legged wooden stand
To keep the thick stone bottom off the ground
Allowing water to slowly work its way through
Removing impurities as water drip, drip, dripped below

While charcoal cleaned away the impurities
Jug by jug was filled and replaced with another
This water was for use in the house above
Cool, clear, and such a delight to drink
The drip room is etched in my memory
What a marvel, when I stop and think

Separator and Old Butter Churn

Two adjoining cattle pens with a gate between
Milking cows locked in one, calves in the other
Separated each night for milk in the morning
Up at five-thirty, we helped milk the cows
First wash the udders, then squeeze the nipples
Always leave enough for the calves to drink
Excited they were, as we opened their gate

Some milk we drank straight from the cow
So fresh and warm—not available now
The rest poured in the old separator bowl
With handle turned round and round
The fluid from the cream removed
Through separate spouts they flowed
One to the pig trough; the other to the butter churn

The cream poured into a two-foot churn
Top covered, the handle plunged up and down
As the butter got thick, we removed the top for a peek
Quite a job for one to do—twenty-five minutes or more
This was in the 1930s when we had no electricity
Manpower was used; we all took turns—
Until cream turned by degree into butter so sweet

Butter then rinsed with water from the dripping stone
Placed on a dish, salted to taste, and stored in the cupboard

—Refrigeration not possible or needed
A slice of baked bread, thick with
Fresh-straight-from-the-cow-oh-so-good butter!
Since my youth, no better butter have I found
So pure, thick, and savory—no longer available today

Bluefields Guest House

At the foot of the hill, a mile from Shafston
Bluefields Guest House rested on a rented property
Peggy, an English lady my father hired to manage it
Boasted of the handsome, eight-large-bedroomed house
Set on a charming property traveled by a small river

Into the house flowed electricity from a hydraulic turbine
My father built to convert river water to energy
Outside, a revitalizing waterfall refreshed eager bathers
Waters so cool and clear; pebbles plain to see,
Tiny fish swam under the overhead breadfruit-tree canopy

Nine-year-old entrepreneur was I
Small, round, toothsome cookies my wares to sell
Bachelor's buttons, they were called
Weekly, three dozen plus a few, baked to perfection
Taken to the guest house on horse they went

Peggy, my only client, served them with tea
The money earned barely filled my piggy bank

A veterinarian and his young daughter visited each year
An only child who knew how to ride horses
I allowed her to show her skills on my Palomino
Years later, the vet arranged for my younger brother
A scholarship to Glasgow University
I am thankful to have known this man

Sir Alexander Bustamante
Prime Minister to be, spent a week at the inn
Fascinated by his thick white hair
My siblings and I would scramble to sit on his knees
From his pocket would spring Paradise Plum sweeties

Rushing home after dark
Bamboo screeching scared us all
Around the corner on a lignum vitae tree
An old owl hooted its two short hoos
The moon caused terrifying shadows to shift
Insects and frogs made their circadian night noises
Fireflies' eyes aglow, a signal to their mates
We galloped home at breakneck speeds
Longing for next week's visit

Nature

My Palomino

A young filly born on the Shafston lands
Enjoyed so much to play and prance
A vicious bull had anger on his mind
It gored this colt in the crotch one day
Wounding it beyond repair

For a gun my father went, the colt to shoot
But I to the baby horse did run
"Daddy put the gun away, I'll care for her
Then she'll be mine"
"Okay my child I will do as you say"
I hugged her close, told her she'd be fine

Patches of red and white
My Palomino was in sight
She knew me at a glance
Then began her usual prance
I nursed her for over a year
There's no greater love affair in any hemisphere

On her rump I would jump
Training her not to be scared
After learning to keep her spirit calm
Into the saddle I climbed
With my hand I patted her on her side
She knew we were going for a ride

The pull of the rein gave her a clue
Gallop through open fields
Under tropical blue skies
Together in the ocean we would swim
Then strode upon the Sabito Beach
Children staring, wishing for a ride

Then to the hills Palo and I would dart
Unlimited land and sky we saw
Watching birds and butterflies go by
In summer, I stood on her back
To reach bunches of guinep
She ate fallen mangos
Chewing seeds and all

We watched cattle driven to the water pond
Horses, mules, pigs and more
Then a side trip to the post office
Mail to collect with bills to pay
A telegram for my mother just arrived
We galloped home to find her waiting there

Palo took me to check bird nests high in the trees
White belly and pea dove, to name a few
Exotic swallowtail hummingbirds flew by
Tody birds, cutest of them all
So tiny, a miracle they are

With shadows moving to the east

Up the hill to Mass Gussie's
Horse-drawn sugar mill
To drink fresh cane juice
While Palo chewed on sugarcane
A moment to reflect on another day's adventure

Patches of red and white
My Palomino was in sight
She knew me at a glance
Then began her usual prance
I nursed her for over a year
There's no greater love affair in any hemisphere

Mules

Did you know
A mule is the offspring
Of a male donkey, a jack
And a female horse, a mare?
Horses have sixty-four chromosomes
Donkeys sixty-two chromosomes
The mule ends up with sixty-three
So can be either male or female
Because of the odd number of chromosomes
The mule cannot reproduce
The mule is more resilient
Than a horse or donkey
It was always used for the hard work on a property

A sure-footed, smooth-riding animal
Caesar crossed the Rubicon on a horse
Jesus chose to enter Jerusalem on a donkey
My father always rode a mule

Seen Things Few Have Ever Seen

Seen things few have ever seen
Seen an old aunt asleep, mouth open wide
A cockroach frolicking on her tongue
Antennae stretching outward
Signaling the great delight
It felt in this damp new home

Seen a ram goat lying on my mother's bed
With large horns he chewed his cud
I went into the room, quickly reversed
Then spread the bad news around
"Call the gardener and all the help"
They moved the ram with much distress

Held the tiny todus bird in my palm
Fingers closed around his oh-so-small body
Not a feather showed—his heart pounding
Opening my fingers—he flew away
Nest knitted to the end of a small branch
Young swayed by the gentle breeze

Father had an alligator in a large cage
Scared were we, but taunted it most days
Loved to hear him bark, his noisy bark
We had chickens that I loved
The gardener fed "Ali" with my red hen
Cried so much my mom put me in her bed

Yes, I've seen a great many things
Few have ever seen

Open Your Eyes

It's paradise. But notice what goes unnoticed
Fun in the sun, carousing all day long
Dancing to the music of Calypso drums
Frolicking under coconut trees

No thought of bald pate feeding her young
A crow picking up crumbs
Secretive, yellow-crowned night heron
A rare opportunity easily missed

Rum and Coke affect neurotransmitters of the brain
Minds twisted toward self-obsessive egomania
No regard for creative entertainment God freely provides
Open your eyes—side effects, a calming peace

What do you see when around crowds?
Or simply walking in the woods?
You could miss the mongoose
Slyly disappearing into a hole at the base of a tree
Or a bald eagle soaring high above

Are you aware of the mockingbird singing
In the black olive tree just outside your door?
Or have you seen the form of a dove in the storm
    clouds
You say, "Who cares about the mockingbird?"
Guess who? Almighty God does

Thank you, Lord, for open eyes

Amazing God I Love

I have been so blessed
I was born in the midst of nature
After forming the earth
You made Adam, then Eve
—You also made me

You gave me the privilege to be close to nature
In a small area of the world
Deep love of all creatures, especially birds
Afforded me a good understanding
Of the perfection of my amazing God

Surrounded by mountains, forests, rivers
Breadfruit, ackee, avocado, and sugarcane, to name a few
Overlooking forty miles of emerald coastal waters
I was never bored—chickens, goats, pigs, and even an alligator
Played games with tiny soldier crabs found under rocks

In a cave not far away, we ate marl off the sides of walls
Parrots in the Amazon eat this stuff too
It protects them from poisonous berries in the forest
I only found this out recently—
Maybe that's why I am alive at eighty-five

Hours roaming forests on foot and horseback with my brothers
I never missed a thing that moved
Snakes, mongoose, hopping-dick birds that hop from one rock to another,
The stunning white-belly dove
Climbed trees to watch birds construct their nests
Observing their young hatch, grow, then fly away

I am in awe
As I reflect on the eyes of the creatures I came to know
Remembering the days of my youth like they were yesterday

Seeing the hand of the amazing God I love
Sharing His creation with me

Alone

Birds that mate for life
To the feeding trees they fly
On the wing, no sign of strife
To fill their craws with choice
Pimento berries—oh-so ripe—
For their young waiting patiently

Across the way, a farmer walks
Gun in hand, smoking his pipe
He hides behind a wooden fence
Minds on their brood back home
So unaware of danger at hand
They slowly fly across the land

Aim taken—a shot came forth
The gun smoked, a cartridge fell
A bird fluttered to the ground
The dog sent to fetch the prize
"My love is down!" She flew away
A single mom was born today

Never to see her mate again
Little ones cared for every day

Only to grow, then go their way
No one to love, not even her own
High up in a tree, there she sits
A solitary soul, singing a in a lonesome tone

After a Hurricane

Outside the grocery store, two days after the storm
Twenty feet from the entrance, in my way
Mama duck and eight ducklings

She stood with half-opened, sleepy eyes
I snapped the shot and stayed watching
Marveling that her young survived the terrible storm
They sat semicircled around her with eyes mostly closed

Customers walking by
She did not move
A chick nudged her with its bill
She did not move

A minute later, she opened one eye—her chicks to check
In a split second it was closed again
She was exhausted
The way we were

Icefield Parkway

Spanning the distance between Jasper and Banff
The number-one scenic drive in North America
Advertising tectonic-impacted megaliths
We drove this Junoesque panorama
Scenes traversing the transcendent Icefield Parkway

Ice dripping from the sides of limestone cliffs
While sulphur springs bubbled and steamed
A distinct sulphur-dioxide smell escaped bubbling hot springs

One side of the road boasted a forest of pine trees
A river in a hurry rushes through the green field below
Taking in these alluring scenes, I stockpiled them in my mind

Turning to the other side, a windblown mountain reached for the sky
Majestic rocks, carved by the elements, framed its face
Eyes ranged across this spectacle—not a green leaf to be seen
Wind, rain, snow, and ice conspired to form this wondrous scene
Although barren and lifeless, the evidence of artistry plainly visible

Continuing on, the landscape quickly changed

A dense, bewitching, mysterious fog rolled toward us
Capturing the visibility to nothing; scared, we stopped
Enveloped in this cloud of fog, concealing the road ahead
We sat contemplating how long we would be in this lonely state

The fog moved on, and so did we, until reaching a rest area
Parking the car, we proceeded to follow a narrow path along a hillside
Capturing on film the curious mountain flora and trickling streams
We saw high on a nearby tree, the fierce beauty of a bald eagle
The great bird—aptly symbolizing the strength and freedom of America

Arriving at the Columbia Icefield, largest icefield in the Canadian Rockies
We embarked on a tour bus, which drove onto an ancient ice-cracked glacier
Buses filled with visitors were balanced precariously on its surface
Walking, I saw narrow cracks exposing an underbelly of baby-blue ice
Years of snow compressed to form a thick mass, unique in its ability to flow

Standing on the Bow Summit, 6,800 feet above sea level, snow had fallen
Leaning against the railing and looking below, I took a sharp breath
Awakened eyes encountered the neon, turquoise Peyto Lake
The most visited and photographed lake in the Canadian Rockies
Glacial rock flour flows into the lake, giving it an iridescent intensity

Thundering waterfalls, spectacular vistas extending for miles
Diverse and unusual scenery have lodged here for millennia
Gold, orange, and pink painted the sky as the sun began to set
Clutching my coat closer, returned to the car and headed for Banff
Truly a wonderland—breathtaking and overflowing with God's attributes

Black Bears (an Icefield Excursion)

Ten-thirty, one quiet June evening, driving a gravel road
The soon-to-set sun dappled through the pine trees
Slamming on the brakes, gravel crackled under tires

Announcing an enormous, black bear guarding the road
She locked her gaze on our car

Tilting her head toward the forest behind
In the bushes on hind legs stood four tiny cubs
Momma checks on us again, then signals with her head
Little ones scampered quickly across to the other side
Waiting until the last had crossed, she slowly followed

Adrenaline coursed to every capillary, heightening our senses
The family disappeared into the thick Alberta forest
All eyes fixed on the sacred space they had faded into—
A release of oxygen; an embrace of a hallowed moment
We had seen a black bear and her cubs in the wild

Un-Nature

Selfie Generation

Have a good night's sleep
Always look your very best
Not a single hair out of place
Makeup to last through the day

Cameras are everywhere—
At the store I asked for help
She briskly took me to the shelf
Turned and looked away

Hands touching her hair
Making sure it was still in place
I thought it odd of her to look away
She was a clerk in this fine store

I was at a loss. "Are you okay?" I asked
"Oh, yes," was her reply, posing
"We are both on camera," she said
As she touched her hair again

"You must always be prepared
Never know when someone will
Want to take a selfie with you
Always smile and look your best"

"Now, if you are through
Can you help me find the ink cartridge?"

She could not find it thereamong
She only knew where the camera hung

I Do Not Understand. Do You?

I cannot fathom the fun a person gets from fishing
Standing in the sun on a bank, hour after hour
Yes, he catches fish—then throws them back!
No regard for the pain he just caused
Yet, if the fisherman feels a slight irritation in his mouth
He is ready to run to the emergency room
Or grab himself a shot of rum
With no mercy for the many fish with swollen jaws

I saw a woman standing over her husband's grave
Hand on her shoulder; I said, "Sorry for your loss"
Turning she shouted, "What the hell are you sorry for?
That son-of-a-b**** [and that was not all]
You don't know what he did!"
I quickly backed away, expecting her to whack me
Thinking it was him come back to haunt her
I got in my car as she continued to curse the corpse

A man standing in the sun, hours on end
A woman at a grave, cursing the dead
I do not understand. Do you?

The Flood

Just sitting around, no TV or Internet
—seven days of rain
Makes me wonder, will it ever end?
I will wait a day or two, hopefully not forty!
And thankfully not with two-of-every-kind

I have placed my mind in a place it used to dwell
A time I never knew that TV and Internet might ever
be invented—and then so missed
It was a lovely time
I never got angry or bent out of shape
Certainly didn't worry about a thing I never knew

On the eighth day, water receding
Turned on the TV just to give it another try
There he was, in full color, some news guy
I almost turned it off...
But didn't
Now a difficult decision—which channel to watch?

Alone, Yet Not Alone

Anxiety fills the air; a virus draws near
Yes, COVID-19 starts with a bang
Fiercely Attack Corona is its name

Stay at home! Wear a mask! Wash hands!
Social's new claim, "Keep your distance!"

I am alone, yet I am not alone
In emptiness is found an unspoken presence
Grabbing the full attention of the mind
Unexpected happens, only if you let it

I did not ask for this silent time
This time to know who I really am
Strengthened by faith, He's here with me
Peace I have found within my being

A virus interrupted my everyday
Yet it's so refreshing to spend this time
Looking past this greedy world
Knowing, although alone, I am not alone

God

One Slip Away

Dancing among the tulips and exotic butterflies
I slipped—He grabbed me by my hair
Dragged me quickly into his arms
I told Him he was hurting my head
"My child, do you know where you nearly fell?"
He held me close as I turned and looked

The slime into which I almost slipped
A deep pit with souls everywhere
Party at one end, people getting stoned without fear
Falling deeper into a sinkhole that sucked them away
That was the miry pit I had read about one day

"Who are you?" I looked into His face. He did not reply
"Why do you care about me?" A tear fell from His eye
He loves me! I was inwardly moved
"You are crying, I must know why you care"

He washed me off and combed my hair
"Come see"
There on a distant hill
Stood that old, rugged cross I had so often read of
Bloodstains created by his pierced side

"You are my precious child," He said
"You will never return that way again

Your soul has been created to follow me
Since the time I knit you together in your mother's womb
My truth is engraved in your soul, so you can never stray"

There was rejoicing at the foot of the cross
Among the faithful who love the lost
It is my goal to serve Him all my days and warn about that slimy pit
I was only one slip away
My Savior lives; He loves us all; His name is Jesus
Come follow Him Today

More Like You

(Sung to any Reggae Tune)

I want to be more like You, Jesus
More like You, more like You
I want to be more like You
For without You, I wander and get lost

Ground me in Your statutes
So my heart will always follow
My life will portray Your likeness
And my lips will sing Your praise

I want to be just like You, my Savior

Lead me on the narrow road
Guide me through the storms I face
Give me peace no one can steal

Endow me with Your wisdom
To interpret Your will as You make clear
Keep me strong in the face of discord
Clean hands and a pure heart I desire

I want to be more like You, Jesus

Storms

Storms in life are sure
As sure as the wind
That blows in as a hurricane
Making its own path

Don't bother run from them
They capture you every time
Enter them, looking—
Seeking the greater lesson

Some things can only be learned
In the midst of storms
—In the midst of storms
With the Lord

Wisdom

I prayed for wisdom
It led me to understanding
God heard my prayer and allotted me my portion
Wisdom has served me well, understanding is my friend
Not so for the foolish; I see the dilemma of these folks
Lives filled with false worldly joys, a blurred highway ahead
Folks my age or older unable to fulfill their empty dreams
Some bedridden for years, others with numerous diseases
Falling, breaking bones, not able to find rest for their souls

Dear Lord, before me, the destiny of all is clear
Suffering is not without merit, when one understands
The power it holds to draw us closer to Your side
Tears fill my eyes when I talk to the aged and show them Your love
They turn away; they do not understand
They suffer in vain, hopeless despair fills their souls
Not understanding You desire their hearts

You have kept me in the palm of Your hand since my youth
Your mercy, love, and wisdom have guided me

through my years
I have always prayed for Your protection when my time should arrive
Now I'm old and diagnosed with lung disease
Because I understand clearly Your love for me
I will embrace the path and purpose wisdom has shown
And hold firm to Your every word as Your mercy fills my soul

All the wisdom of God is found in Christ Jesus, my Lord

The Old Master and His Masterpiece

Life is but a large canvas painting
Every brushstroke illustrates beauty—or not
Mistakes will be made
How they are corrected is what matters
Selfish ambition and greed
Mar the canvas

The thing about this painting—
A start over is not possible
Consider carefully your trek through life
It is equal to the stroke of the brush, which cannot be erased
Contemplate each stroke before you move the brush

Have God hold your hand
Then your brushstrokes will be perfected in Him

Each day, a unique stroke
Texture
Fluidity
Color
Mistakes—He blends into new vistas

He, the Old Master; you, His masterpiece
Let your canvas erupt with the presence of Jesus!

Unfolding Rosebud

You are a beautiful rosebud, so lovely to behold
Can you unfold your petals without tearing them apart?
Try as you may, you are just not able
The secret of unfolding this bud is known to God alone
So do not try to unfold your life outside of His plan
In Him, you are perfectly and wonderfully made

I pray you will allow Him to mold you into His image
And like the rose, continue to blossom in His everlasting love
A rose-laden bush is a delight to the eyes and food for the mind

And like the strong, sweet smell of this lovely flower
Surround yourself with the essence of His love
And watch as He unfolds the seamless bud of your life

My friend, as you travel on your journey through life
Keep the Word always hidden in your heart
Spend time with folks who do not suppress His truth
Love others with the love of Christ our Lord
And listen for God's voice as He whispers in your ear
"This is the way; walk in it, and you will find rest for
    your soul"

Knitting

I see God's work in my life since the time
He knitted me together in my mother's womb
Choosing the correct stitches, He places them on my
    heart
He put needles in my hands, instructing me to knit
Now stitch with Me as I guide you each and every day

At the end of each row, we do a knit or a pearl
Turning the corner of my in-progress garment
He guides my heart as I knit another row
My mind wanders; I drop a stitch or two
He points out my error, showing me how to mend

I soon mess up again, dropping many stitches

That go rows below; grabbing the needles
He teaches me self-control, patience, and a clear mind
Following his instructions, I slip them safely back in
　　place
Dropped stitches now secured, I knit on

Looking back at the pattern of this my life
I see clearly how He knitted me together
When my knitted life is over and neatly folded
My Savior will be waiting at heaven's door
I will enter wearing this knitted robe He made with
　　me

Follow His instructions exactly—He'll help you too

Redeeming Grace, I Could Not Claim

Redeeming grace, I could not claim
Yet, He kept watch over me as I grew
I sensed Him and sometimes turned away
Still He washed the scales from my eyes
At a hill far away on a wooden cross
He entered my soul with a mighty rush

He took me on a high mountaintop
I marveled at the glory of His creation
He focused me on the steep path from which I came
Over the edge were the cliffs I climbed

Sharp edges of rocks had wounded me
Never again do I want this path to see

On the other side of this mountaintop
Was the straight and narrow path I should have taken
I had been blind and could not see
The road that would lead me to His side
He took me to the cross, wounds washed away
Then said, "Go show your friends this narrow way"

Friends, and all who want to hear!
Come join and walk along this road
He walks this path with me each day
He is there waiting to welcome you
He watches over me and will never leave
He will do the same for you, my friends
If only you will cleave

Growing Old

Legs

I used to think I had lovely legs
Not too fat, not too thin
Legs girls would be jealous of
But that was a long time ago

Watched the old ladies as they sat
I didn't understand why
Their legs were so out of shape and fat
Mine will never be like that!

Now my legs are eighty-five
The tune they sing, a different one—
Sun blotches, red and brown
Swollen feet that touch the ground

"Exercise," the doctor commands
I venture out for a short walk
And tell them to move—they answer, "No!"
Leading me home, they start to swell

Now I am the old lady sitting around
I loved my legs when I was young
And now I love them even more
Grateful for the life they walked for me

Thank you; Lord, they still can dance!

Glacial Flow (Slowing Down)

I visited the Hubbard Glacier many years ago
Some one hundred and seventy miles long
With glacial flow, it moves one meter each day
I was young, and speed was all I knew
Get things done, and quickly, was the way
Glacial movement was not part of my day

Today my legs transport me at glacial flow
I'm thankful for this diminished movement
The alternative—"no flow"—is not desired
So I will move my limbs as long as I can
And thank my God for these legs of mine
They have served me well through time

Lungs

My lungs now rebellious
Looking for the attention my legs captured
"Don't leave us behind!
We're weary and tired," they shout
I turn to my heart and command
"Don't join the mutinous two!"
Now my heart has had to step in
Serving both legs and lungs too!

The Dripping Faucet

Surgery on my leg, a carcinoma
After waiting more than an hour
I watched as the doctor got the knife
Seeming to enjoy her life—
She removed inches of my flesh
"Return in two weeks, stitches to remove"
She smiled

At home the blood gushed
Down my leg, into my shoe and on the floor
Back to the doctor I was taken
Rebandaged as she had before
"Have a bath, but don't get it wet!"

How do I do that? I pondered
It's a carcinoma; I don't want it spreading
A quick shower it has to be!
Be careful
Stand on one leg in the shower
Lift the other high
Remember I am almost eighty-six

Two days later at the pulmonologist
For a breathing examination
But that was not the real test!
I was an hour in the waiting room
When the nurse opened the door
"It's your turn now"

Down the passage to the left
"What's your birth, height, weight, meds"
She left the room and closed the door
With leg hurting and lungs quite out of breath
I sat and waited, hoping for the best

Another hour, I was frustrated
I made my way to the door
Looked down the passageway
No one in sight
Exhausted, I sat back down

My brain told me I was in captivity
There was nothing I could do
Stuck, I watched a dripping water faucet
Drip, drip, drip
Water!
At least I won't die immediately

My mind wondered back to Havana
—My 1959 tour of the city
And the dungeons
Dark, damp, drip, drip, drip
Castro's poor victims
Who later waited there
Waiting, waiting, waiting

POWs—all over the world

In foreign countries
Locked in hell
I prayed asking God's care on them

Gradually, a change in my disposition
The nurse returned in great contrition
I gave a "No problem" with a patient smile

From that time on, when tempted toward impatience
I remember the suffering and dying
Of those who would stave off our captivity

Forgive me for my complaining of these mild frustrations
I'll stop wasting time, and pray on all occasions

Teach Us, Nuh Man!

Your many years have been so good to you
Tell us your secrets; we want to share them too
Was it the sugarcane that made you so strong?
Or cockpit country coffee that kept you all along?

Was it saltfish and ackee, or breadfruit and yam?
We want to know, please tell us—yah man!
Could it have been curry goat or delicious curry ram?
Banana fritters or even you granny's sorrel jam?

You pass de doctor office and you give it not a glance
Please, tell us what keeps you from his trance?
De doctor even waves, wishing you would come around
You answer, "Listen here, Doc, I don't need you ultrasound"

Friend, our money's on you to pass the one-hundred mark
Leaving Bob Hope's record completely in the dark

Reflect on Him

Don't even try to imagine getting old without the Lord
I'm not what I used to be; everything is giving in
I reflect on the days of my energy and strength
There was nothing I could not do
Now there is not that much that I can do

Why does the Lord want me to fall apart?
Why not take me now instead of later?
Each day is getting more difficult
I tell my legs to move. They answer, "No"
How did I ever do the things I used to do?

He answers me in the silence of the night
"I want you now to carefully reflect on Me
Your work on earth is not complete

I want you to be ready when I call your name
So be an example of love, joy, peace and self-control"

His purpose is clear: He wants you and me, my friends
To examine our lives daily as we go
Time is running out for some of us
Be encouraged and turn to Him now
Receive His salvation
And rejoice that you will see His face one day

Outro

This poem was written during the 1950s by Dorothy's husband, Kenneth Rizk Mahfood, to whom she was married just shy of fifty-five years. It is a fitting way to end Dorothy's collection of poems.

The Rose

The rose that springs
From least of which it should,
Makes first of all a brilliant flourish
Then fades, from lack of nourishment to nothingness
At first when beauty glistens from its limbs,
One forgets the lurking fate to which it's doomed
And only marvels at its present radiancy.
And then the passing of the time,
The sun—the drought—the rain conspire
To bring ruin unto this lovely flower.
At times, the powers of the earth
That make and ruin with one accord
Show preference to one ill-fortuned flame:
And 'though its life is lengthened but a while
To the very end, it's all the same.
A rose is born; a rose has died;
And between is but a passing thought.

—Kenneth Rizk Mahfood

Inspired by Dorothy's Life

If you enjoyed Dorothy's poetic memoir, on the following page, you can read Chapter 1 of Dale Mahfood's historical fiction novel, *Oristano*. Dale has written the first of *The Jamaica Chronicles* series, a coming-of-age, fictionalized retelling of a year in his mother's life. You'll recognize some events and themes found in *A Simple Smile*, along with many rich fictional characters and events. *Oristano* is a must-read for those who enjoy family sagas and historical fiction.

Encourage Others to Read "A Simple Smile"

If you found *A Simple Smile* a worthwhile read, encourage others to read it by going online to the bookseller or library you received this book from and writing a quick review. It doesn't have to be long and fancy. Just write the same thing you'd tell your friend about the book.

Oristano

by Dale Mahfood

CHAPTER 1
1972

"All happy families resemble one another, each unhappy family is unhappy in its own way."
—Leo Tolstoy

Cailin wept. She wasn't sure of all the reasons. Maybe she cried because no one else did. Or maybe because of unrecognized tension bottled up inside her over the last forty-one years. One thing she knew for sure—she cried because she loved him. And today, standing by her father's grave, she was his little girl again. Thoughts swirled through her mind of times she vied for his attention with a silly joke or dance. She longed for that chance again, but it was too late. It had been too late for a long time.

The others drifted away from the graveside, walking back to the house. Only she and Archie remained, gazing down the slope past the lush lower foothills and on to the many layered hues of the blue Caribbean bay.

Sharpe, her father's property foreman, stood in the midday sun at a respectful distance. Dark skinned and neatly dressed in a starched, timeworn white shirt and black pants, he watched sentinel over the grave.

"How long has it been since you've been back?" asked Archie.

Cailin's only reply was silence.

He tried again. "I've been gone so long, I forgot on a beautiful day like today the view seems to stretch from Black River to Negril Point. It really is breathtaking."

Again, no response.

He looked at her thoughtfully, then said, "The innocent, fair-haired girl I met years ago hasn't changed a bit—except, of course, for the benefits age brings a few fortunate individuals." He looked her up and down. "Your style reminds me of the women back in New York. I guess the big-city Kingston lifestyle suits you." He smiled.

Cailin returned a smirk—*ever the sweet mouth*—and turned to walk the short distance to the old silk cotton tree, Archie trailing behind.

The cotton tree lay partially by the gravel road with the bulk of its elongated, leafless branches stretching down the mountain slope. It was said to have been the oldest and largest silk cotton tree in all the Caribbean. Now, it lay without interment close to her father's unmarked grave. The still-well-planted, stubborn roots of the massive, tentacled stump were as high as six feet above the ground at some points. When Cailin was younger, the maids would tell her ghosts—or what they called "duppies"—lived in between the cotton tree roots. She wondered with a smile if the roots were now her father's haunt. That was the first lighthearted thought she'd had since her sister had called her two days earlier telling her of her father's death.

Leaning against a root, with her eyes still moist, she sighed, then finally spoke. "It's been sixteen years since I last came up here. I wanted him to meet his grandchildren." She looked over to Archie. "But you know Daddy. It was a brief meeting." She paused, and with a smile, continued, "but not as brief as when Rand asked him for permission to marry me. Daddy met us with a shotgun, yelling at Rand, saying he would never allow me to marry an Arab."

Archie laughed. "Sounds like Malcolm. I remember when he wanted to usher me into manhood, to use his terminology. He had a certain lady of the evening, another one of his sayings, come over to Oristano Inn."

Cailin, rolling her eyes, responded, "Spare me the details, please." Remembering Archie in his youth—

smooth words and a thick head of brown hair—there was no need to imagine the evening ladies loving him. His hair was no longer thick, but his words were just as smooth.

Her thoughts returned to her father and involuntarily escaped through her lips. "You know I adored him?"

He laughed and replied, "Everyone knew that! I remember the first day I met you. When I asked you your name, you proudly said you were Cailin Campbell, Malcolm Campbell's daughter. It was like he was the governor of Jamaica."

That made her laugh. "Did I really say that?"

"You did. Just like that."

"I guess I did, then." She looked back out to the sea, then turned to him. "I was surprised to see you here. Last I heard, you took a job with a newspaper in New York."

"Talk about surprised." He reacted like a match lit on fire. "How do you think I felt when I answered the phone at work to the operator saying, 'There's an Irma Campbell on the phone for you. Should I put her through?' She was the last person I expected to hear from. She told me she didn't want me to come, but Malcolm insisted." He looked in Cailin's eyes. "He wanted me here. So, like I always do, I came running." He shook his head. "Anyway," Archie took her arm, "Come, I think we should head back to the house. We'll be missed."

She turned to look at the run-down great house, once the pride of the property. "I really don't want to go back in there...with Irma. Even though today's the first day I've ever met her—his third wife! I don't care for her demeanor, and I can't stand the pleasantries, pretending everything's fine between us—especially at a time like this. For all we know, she could have killed him."

"I wouldn't put it past her, but I don't think so. When I got here last week, the doctor told me the old man's liver was giving out on him." Encouraging her on toward the house, he continued, "I'm sure it won't be long before Irma sells off all Malcolm's property and heads back to Austria, leaving nothing for the family."

"Let's not talk about money," she urged, walking ahead of him. "It's the last thing on my mind today."

"I'm sure you're the only one who feels that way, especially since Malcolm took everyone off the will, except Irma." He caught up to her. "As a matter of fact, did you notice Ian and Gus didn't come to the graveside?"

"Yes, I've been wondering where they've been."

"Malcolm's lawyer gave Ian a tip."

"Mr. Washburn?" She looked at him with a furrowed brow. "What advice did he give Ian?"

"He told him Malcolm had money hidden in the ceiling above his bed. So, he and Gus stayed back to check while Irma was at the graveside."

She stopped in her tracks. "Washburn told Ian that?"

"Yes."

She took a deep breath and continued walking. "Archie, I really don't want to talk about money or the will. He was just put in the grave. Let him rest. At least for a while."

"All right. I won't mention it again. Anyway, you're sure to hear about it." Cailin didn't respond, feigning disinterest.

They found the others sitting at the old, long dining room table talking politely to Irma. Cailin looked at her sisters, brother, and cousin, and her mind took her back thirty years earlier when they would sit at that very table—old as it was then, yet polished and patinated—her father seated at the head, Auntie Abum at the other end. But Irma sat at the head, old and stoic like the now dry, worn-out table, only responding with curt nods and occasional commands to the maid.

Cailin slid into a chair beside Ian and whispered, "Do Rowena and Heather know what you and Gus were up to?"

He leaned his head over. "We didn't find money, like Washburn said there'd be. But we did find something."

"What?" She looked at him.

"Just some old letters. They're addressed to Auntie Abum from the old man's parents."

"What are you going to do with them?"

"If I'd know what they were, I'd have left them up there. Why? Do you want them?"

"Yes. It may be a chance to learn more about Daddy."

"They're yours, then. I put them in my car. I'll give them to you when we leave."

She squeezed his hand and gave him a smile. "Thanks."

Cailin looked over at Irma as she barked a command at the maid to put more lemon in the lemonade and thought it fitting her gray-haired bun was so securely wound that it appeared to pull at the skin on her face, giving her a taut, excruciating appearance. She wondered what her father ever saw in her.

When she could bear the charade no longer, Cailin looked over to Rowena, Rowena looked at Heather, and, as if reading each other's thoughts, the three sisters rose. One by one, from the eldest to the youngest sibling and then their cousin, Gus, they approached Irma and shook her hand. Duty done, they headed toward the front door, leaving their past behind.

Cailin, realizing she may never see Cawdor again, stole out the back-veranda doors to take one last look at the view she had taken for granted in her early years. The distant incoming ocean tide crashed against the barrier reef, foaming toward the shore. She closed her eyes. Memories from the past flooded in. She could hear as if it were yesterday—Malcolm's voice yelling at someone, anyone, during one of his tirades. A bubble formed in her throat. She held it back, deciding she'd done enough crying for one day.

She walked back down the hallway leading through the center of the house toward the front door. With each room she passed, her heart was awash with fluctuating emotions, flowing with bliss and ebbing with apprehension—her family around the supper table filling every seat with laughter and conversation; nights she and Rowena lay in their beds sharing secrets their father could never be allowed to hear; times she, Ian, or Gus were beaten for some infraction of her father's law. Again, a bubble formed in her throat. She swallowed hard, determined not to let Irma get the satisfaction of her tears.

She stepped onto the barbeque, a large, square cement slab almost the width of the main house and more than the depth of the kitchen house. In her youth it had been used to sun-dry pimento seeds, one of her father's business ventures that helped make him the wealthy man he once was.

She met Ian at her car, where he handed her a bundle of old, stained letters bound with yellowed yarn.

She thanked him and gave him a goodbye kiss on the cheek.

When they had all said their goodbyes, Cailin

spotted Sharpe standing by her car. Walking toward him, he opened the driver door to her 1971 Camaro.

"Thank you, Sharpe. This time, you ride in the front seat. We'll make Archie ride in the back. Bring his ego down a bit."

Sharpe chuckled. "If you say so, Miss C."

He closed her door and made his way to the passenger side.

Sitting back in the bucket seat, Cailin put the letters on the console and allowed her shoulders to sink.

Sharpe sat in the passenger seat.

"I don't think I ever told you, but I always appreciated the way you ran the property and especially how you managed my father." She smiled. "He was a lot to manage. How you put up with him, I'll never know."

"Hmm." Sharpe reflected, "The beginning was tough. And sometimes me thought either he would fire me or me would fire myself. But eventually, when me got to understand Busha and him understand me, we was all right."

She looked over at his aging face.

"In the end, when him give up on the property a few years back, him did want make sure say me and Essie was set, so him arrange up with the owner of Oristano Inn to let we run the inn. The place was a sure mess. Nothing like when Archie mother, Miss Gracie, did run it. But between Essie good cooking and me fixing up the place, the guest them start to come back again. Truth is, if it wasn't for Busha…"

Before his eulogy on Busha was complete, Archie opened the passenger door and exclaimed, "You are the man now, Sharpe! You can come back and restore this place to its former glory!"

"Who, me? No, sir! My time at Cawdor done!" Sharpe got out and pulled the seat forward so Archie could get in the back."

"Yes," Archie responded, "you did your time."

"Well…once I would have put it that way, Mass Archie, but now I think forward better than backward."

"You mean forward in the sense of leaving Busha behind." Archie laughed.

"Archie," Cailin moaned. "Not today."

Sharpe and Archie were polar opposites—one tall and dark with low-cut hair, the other medium and light with unkempt, wavy hair. In her youth, Cailin had admired them both for different reasons. Sharpe was pensive and respectful; Archie was sociable and cavalier. It was odd for her to be driving with both in the same car.

It took a full ten minutes to make it slowly down the rough, white-limestone gravel road leading from the Cawdor great house to Oristano. The sloping, cow-populated fields—currently absent of cattle and not even visible because of the overgrown bushes—had previously been well maintained to greeting-card perfection. The low, almost-flawless stone walls that lined both sides of the meandering Cawdor road were now crumbling with gaps every so often, aiding in the erosion of parts of the road. The threesome bemoaned the loss of its beauty, wishing the property could have been seamlessly passed on to one of Malcolm's children before he was too old to manage it. But they knew they were speaking in could-never-have-beens.

At the bottom of the road, the car turned left onto a pothole-hampered road and traveled a quarter mile to a gate with a winding driveway that led to the Oristano Inn. Even though it was not as pristine as Archie and Cailin remembered, both agreed it still held its old charm, partially because of the impressive mountain backdrop.

Cailin pulled under the porte-cochère and stopped.

Picking up the bundle of letters, she got out of the car while Archie remarked from the back seat, "You know I would have opened the door for you, had I not been sitting in the back seat."

She laughed. "Yes,"

"It's second nature," Archie responded as he climbed out from the back seat. "Living and working at the inn honed many a skill—valet, errand boy, chauffeur for drunks. Need I say more?"

"No," Cailin replied, not sure how else to respond.

They walked through the double doors and

climbed the mahogany stairwell.

"Hmm, something smells good!" remarked Archie.

"Is Essie curry goat. She make me buy one once she know say Miss C coming for lunch today."

"Well, I've been here for over a week, and nobody made me curry anything!" teased Archie.

"You will have to take that up with Essie. Besides, you know say she was the chief cook up at Cawdor when Miss C was a girl."

Archie put his hand on Sharpe's shoulder. "You're just taking up for your wife. I remember those days when I came up to the house, you could be found hovering around the kitchen like a John Crow, hoping Essie would pay you some mind,"

Sharpe laughed and nodded his head. "Well, the John Crow get him prize. He gestured toward the balcony. "Come, make we go sit on the balcony and Essie can bring us something to drink."

He called out for Essie, then moved three muleskin planter chairs from the gallery onto the spacious balcony that covered the width of the porte-cochère. Drained from the day's trouble, the three sat facing the bay in the inn's shade.

No one said a word until Essie came out to pay her respects.

"Miss Cailin," Essie took Cailin's hand, "I couldn't bear to see Mass Malcolm put in the grave."

Cailin looked up at her, noticing she had aged

well. "I know, I know, Essie."

Essie went on expressing her sorrow until Sharpe tactfully interrupted, "Essie, why you don't bring some of that nice ginger-cane juice you make this morning."

"Yes." She released Cailin's hand. "Let me go get it."

"None for me, Miss Essie, I'll have my usual rum and Coke. After all, what better way to honor the dead." Archie raised his hand and made a toast. "To Malcolm! In his next life, may it be done unto him what he did unto others." Then he drank down his imaginary beverage.

Cailin heaved a sigh. She had seen Archie like this before, but only after a few drinks. Having to be with Malcolm in his dying days must have been harder on him than she suspected. Now that it was all over, the temporary emotional blockade he constructed was dislodged.

Sharpe leaned forward, turning to Archie. "You sure you need liquor, Mass Archie?"

"Yes!" he said in a commanding tone. Then in the same manner, "I have a question for you, Sharpe. Do you think Malcolm did it?"

"Did what?"

"Do you think he killed that man?"

Sharpe was visibly shaken. "Well...well, I don't...know. There was talk of him killing him. But...but I couldn't say yes or no."

Not liking the direction of the conversation, Cailin jumped in, "You know, Archie, we're all upset. But at least you spent time around him over the last few years. That's more than I got."

Archie turned to face her. "Believe me. It's been no winning day at the racetrack." He turned back toward the bay. "The only reason I ever tried with him is because of my mother. The elegant Gracie Price," he said with sarcasm. "She's still pining for him. All these years living in New York, and she can't forget him." Archie got up and walked over to the baluster, placing his hands on it. Leaning forward, he chastised himself, "And me! At my age, I'm still doing what the old woman tells me. That's the only reason I'm here."

Cailin dropped her head and played with the yarn on the letter bundle.

There was a dense silence until Essie reappeared with the drinks.

Looking at them, Essie interrogated, "What is going on here? All of you have puss on you face. I know Busha dead, but these is the times to tell stories about him, not to fret you self."

Sharpe broke the threesome's silence. "Essie is right, you know. We all have our own stories about Busha, and it look to me like it might do us some good to tell them—the bad and the good."

Archie still at the baluster turned around to receive his drink. "My flight's not for a couple more days, and I have nothing special on my itinerary."

Cailin sat there fingering the letters.

"Miss C?" Sharpe inquired gently. "What about you?"

She hesitated, then replied, "I could call home and let Rand know I won't be back today."

Then she pulled the bow, loosening the yarn from the letters.

To find out more about *Oristano: Book One of The Jamaica Chronicles*, go to DaleMahfood.com.

www.ingramcontent.com/pod-product-compliance
Lightning Source LLC
Chambersburg PA
CBHW030911080526
44589CB00010B/252